SCIENCE WORK

T0100837

THE ROCK FACTORY

THE STORY ABOUT THE ROCK CYCLE

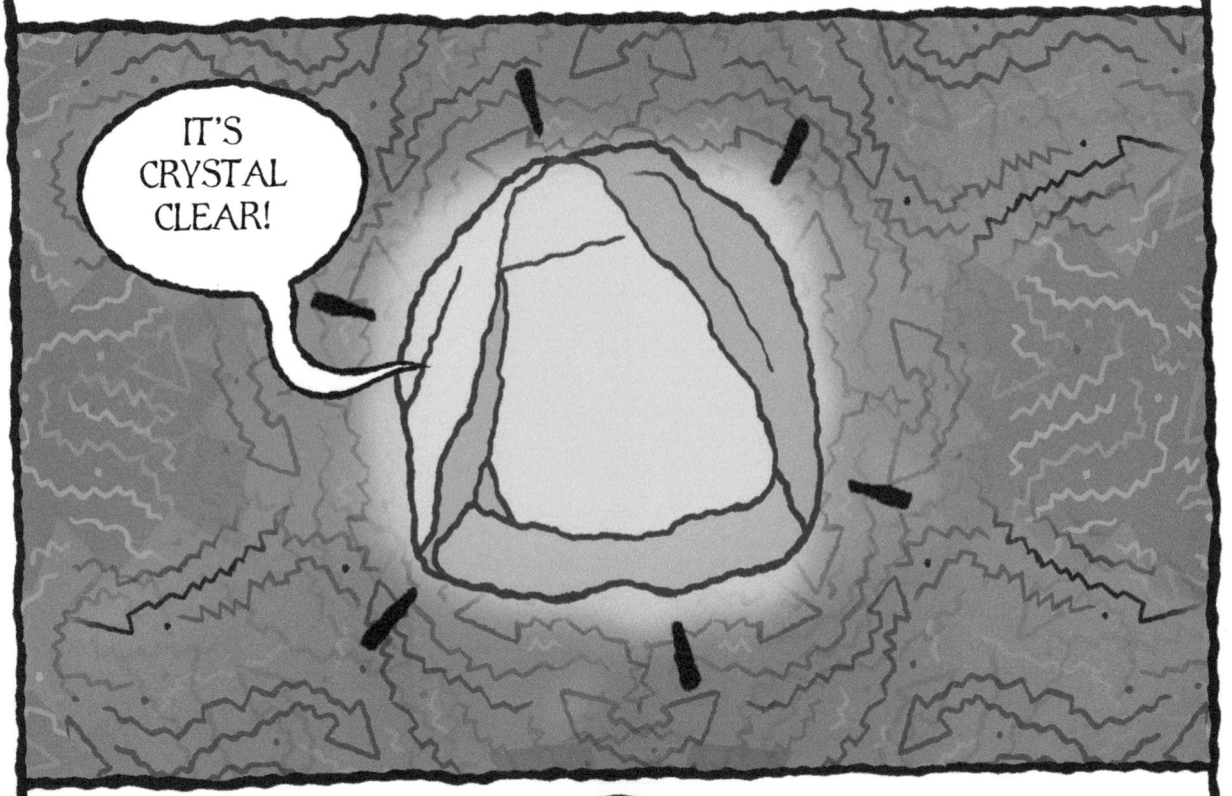

Jacqui Bailey  Matthew Lilly

Picture Window Books • Minneapolis Minnesota

Editor: Jacqueline A. Wolfe
Page Production: Brandie E. Shoemaker
Creative Director: Keith Griffin
Editorial Director: Carol Jones

First American edition published in 2006 by
Picture Window Books, a Capstone imprint
1710 Roe Crest Drive
North Mankato, MN 56003
www.capstonepub.com

First published in Great Britain by
A & C Black Publishers Limited
37 Soho Square, London W1D 3QZ
Copyright © Two s Company 2003

All rights reserved. No part of this book may be reproduced without written permission from the publisher. The publisher takes no responsibility for the use of any of the materials or methods described in this book, nor for the products thereof.

Library of Congress Cataloging-in-Publication Data
Bailey, Jacqui.
The rock factory: a story about the rock cycle / by Jacqui Bailey ; illustrated by Matthew Lilly. p. cm. — (Science works)
Includes bibliographical references and index.
ISBN 978-1-4048-1596-4 (hardcover)
ISBN 978-1-4048-1997-9 (paperback)
1. Petrology—Juvenile literature. 2. Geochemical cycles—Juvenile literature. I. Lilly, Matthew, ill.

II. Title.
QE432.2.B348 2006
552—dc22 2005030011

Printed in the United States 5677

For Louis
JB

For Phil and Alex
ML

Special thanks to our advisers for their expertise, research, and advice:

Dr. Robin Armstrong, Peter Tandy, and Charlotte Stockley
Mineralogy Department at the Natural History Museum
London, England

Larry M. Browning, Ph.D., Professor
Physics Department South Dakota State University
Brookings, South Dakota, USA

Susan Kesselring, M.A., Literacy Educator
Rosemount—Apple Valley—Eagan (Minnesota) School District

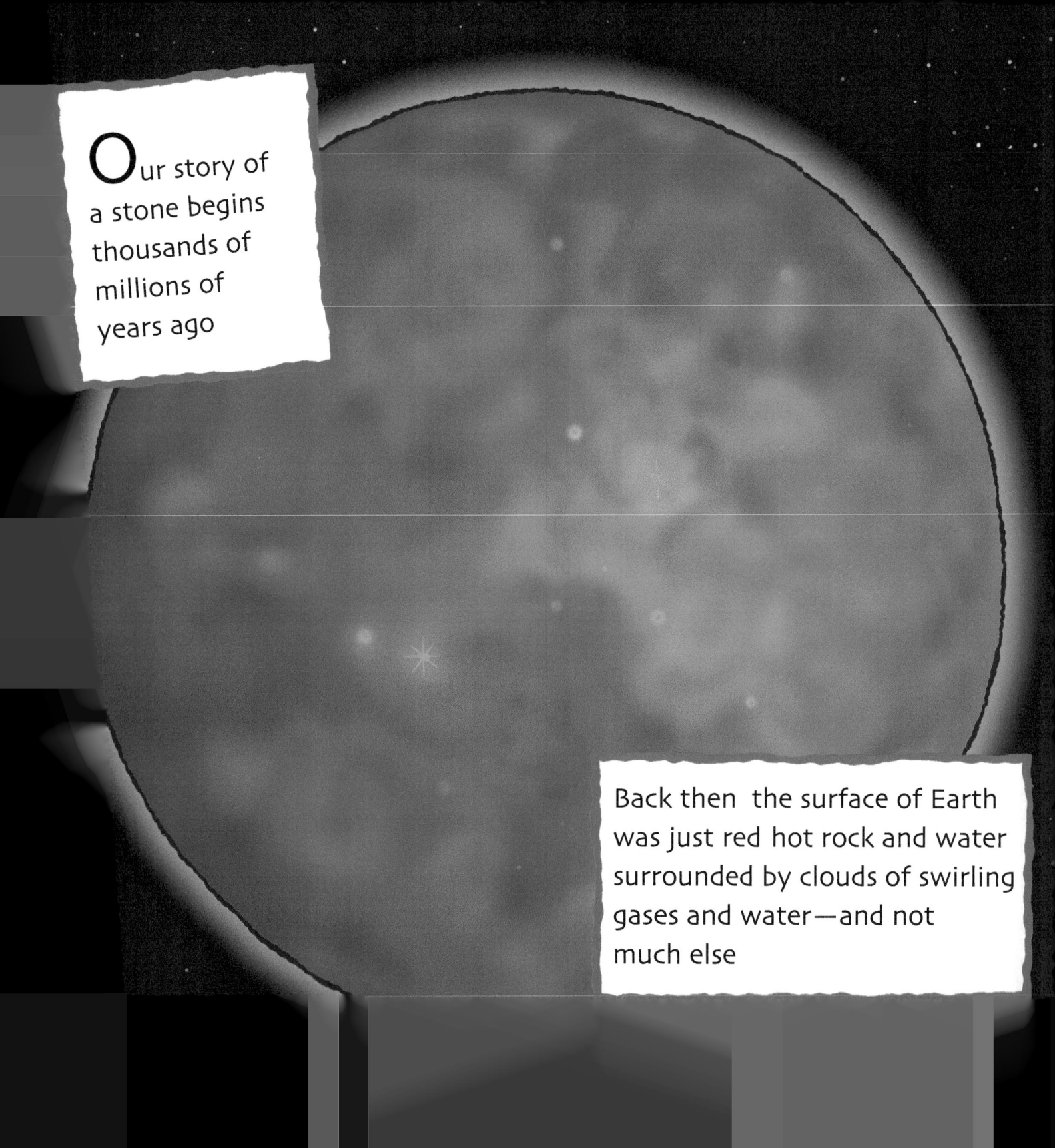

Our story of a stone begins thousands of millions of years ago

Back then the surface of Earth was just red hot rock and water surrounded by clouds of swirling gases and water—and not much else

There were no plants or animals The only things that moved were the wind water and rivers of hot rock from exploding volcanoes
The rivers of rock were escaping from the rock factory deep inside Earth

Our planet is mostly made of rock but it isn't solid all the way through It's made up of different layers like a soft boiled egg
The top layer is the crust This thin layer of hard rock is like the shell of an egg The crust covers all of Earth The land we live on is part of it and the oceans fill the low parts of the crust
HMMM, I'M FEELING A LITTLE CRUSTY TODAY!

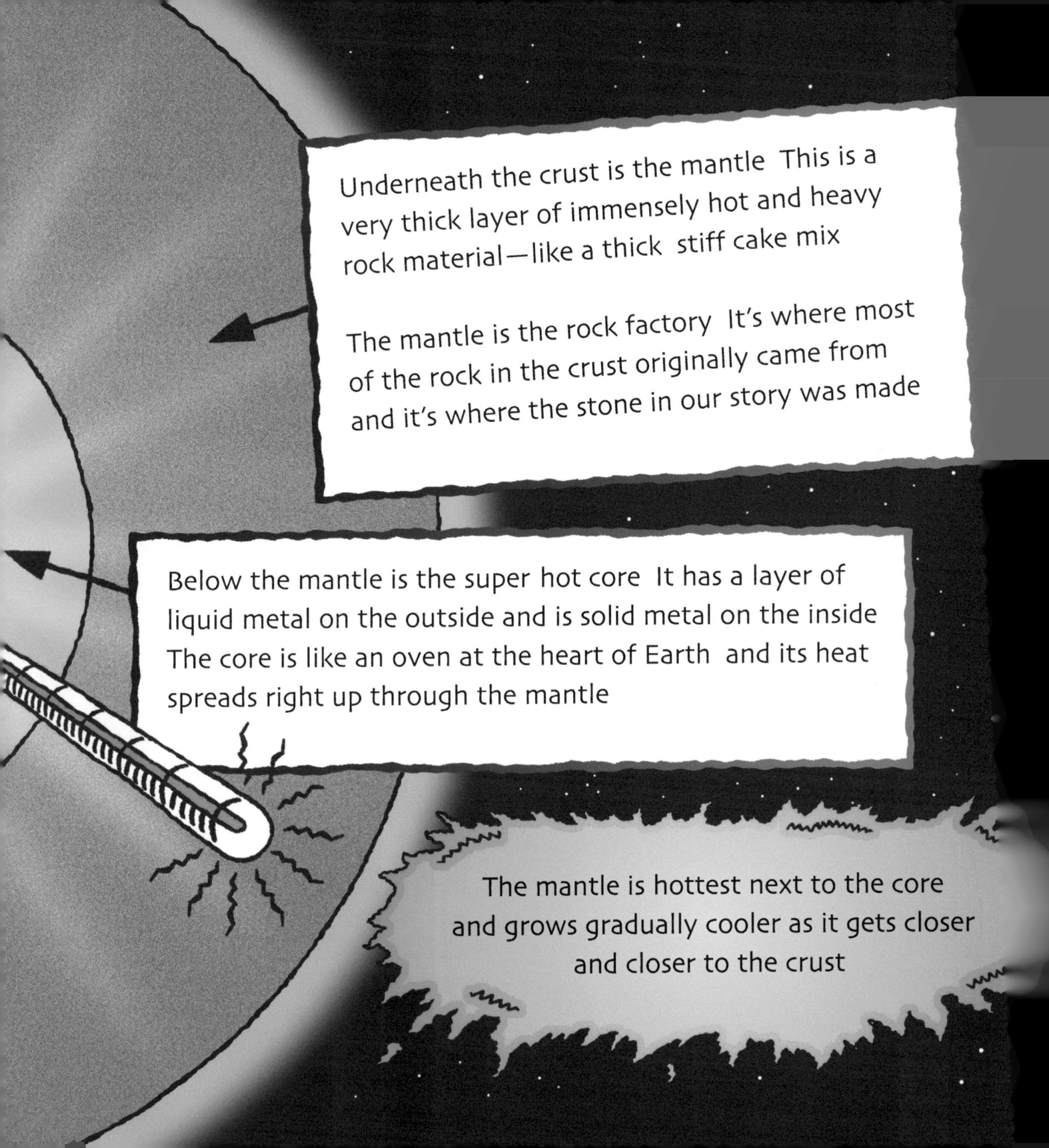

Underneath the crust is the mantle This is a very thick layer of immensely hot and heavy rock material—like a thick stiff cake mix

The mantle is the rock factory It's where most of the rock in the crust originally came from and it's where the stone in our story was made

Below the mantle is the super hot core It has a layer of liquid metal on the outside and is solid metal on the inside The core is like an oven at the heart of Earth and its heat spreads right up through the mantle

The mantle is hottest next to the core and grows gradually cooler as it gets closer and closer to the crust

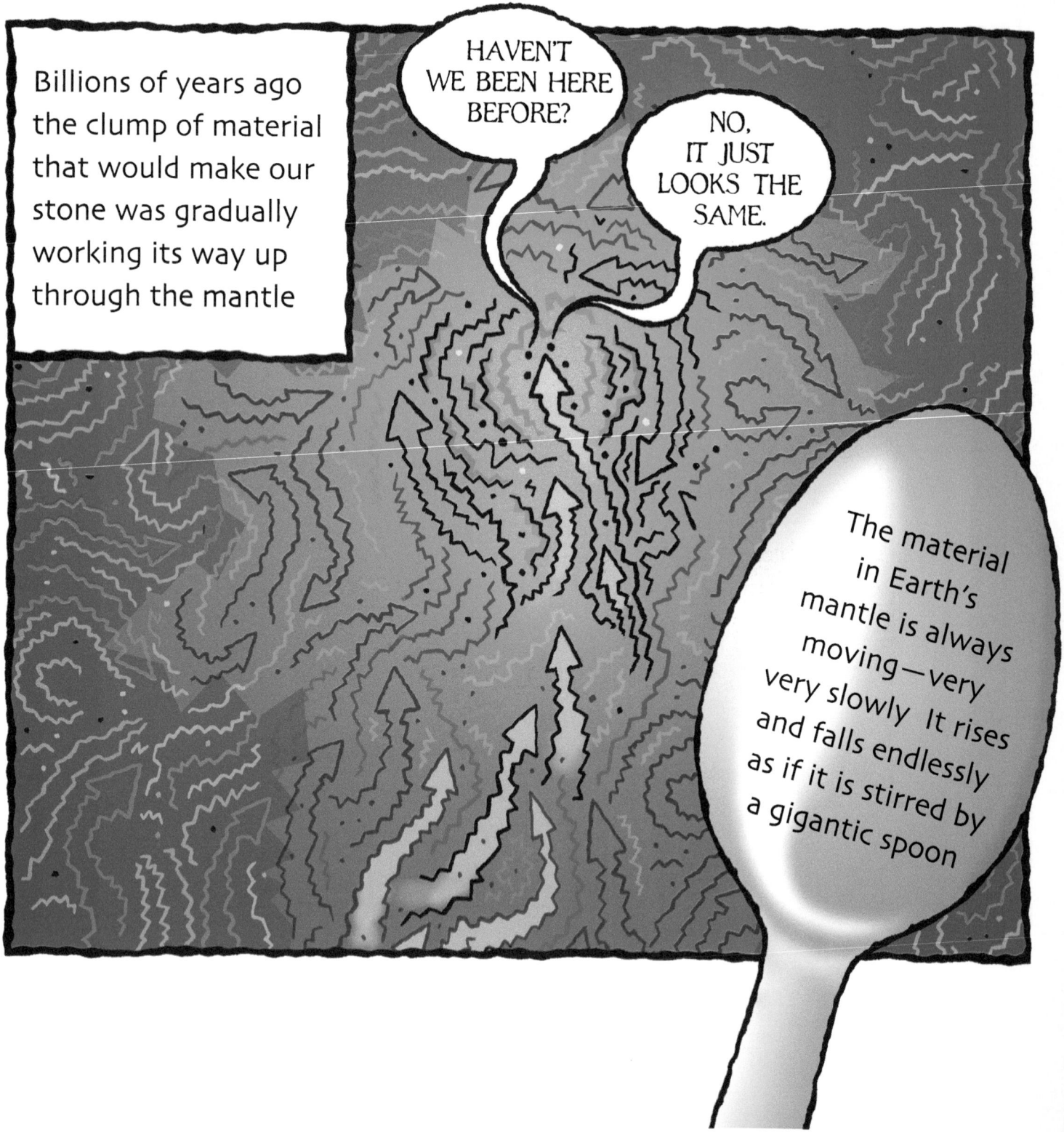
Billions of years ago the clump of material that would make our stone was gradually working its way up through the mantle
HAVEN'T WE BEEN HERE BEFORE?
NO, IT JUST LOOKS THE SAME.
The material in Earth's mantle is always moving—very very slowly It rises and falls endlessly as if it is stirred by a gigantic spoon

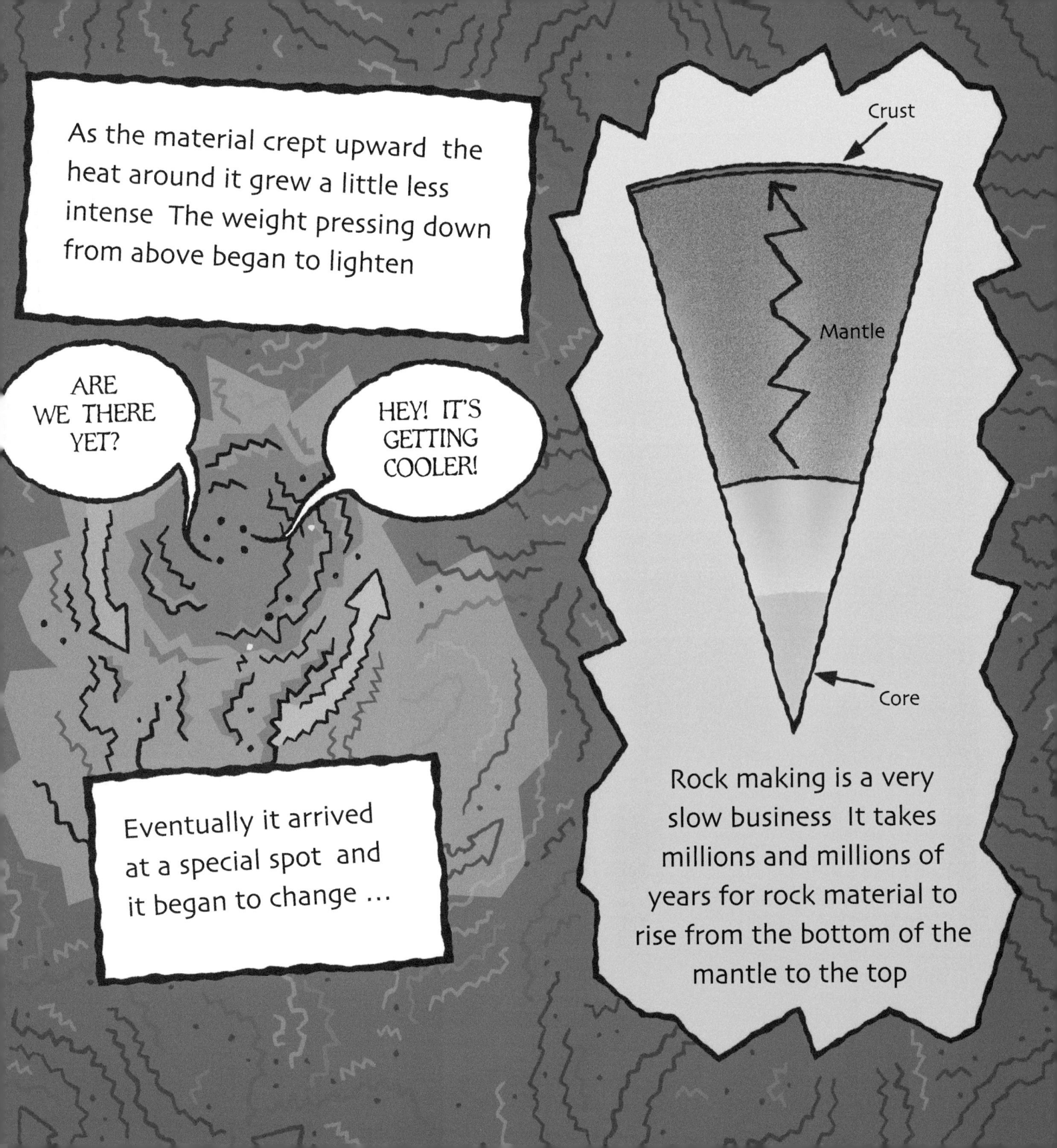
As the material crept upward the heat around it grew a little less intense The weight pressing down from above began to lighten
ARE WE THERE YET?
HEY! IT'S GETTING COOLER!
Eventually it arrived at a special spot and it began to change ...
Crust
Mantle
Core
Rock making is a very slow business It takes millions and millions of years for rock material to rise from the bottom of the mantle to the top

Our clump of material had reached just the right place in the mantle for it to turn into a stone
Most minerals turn into crystals but only when the pressure (caused by the weight of the rocks above them) and the temperature (level of heat) are exactly right for that type of mineral
How does that happen? Well it goes something like this
HEY! WHAT'S HAPPENING?
HELP!
Rock is made from stuff called minerals There are lots of different kinds of minerals and they all shift and stir around in the mantle like the ingredients in a cake mix
As minerals get closer to the crust they begin to cool As they cool they harden into special flat sided shapes called crystals

Each kind of mineral forms its own type of crystal—and when lots of crystals lock together they make rocks

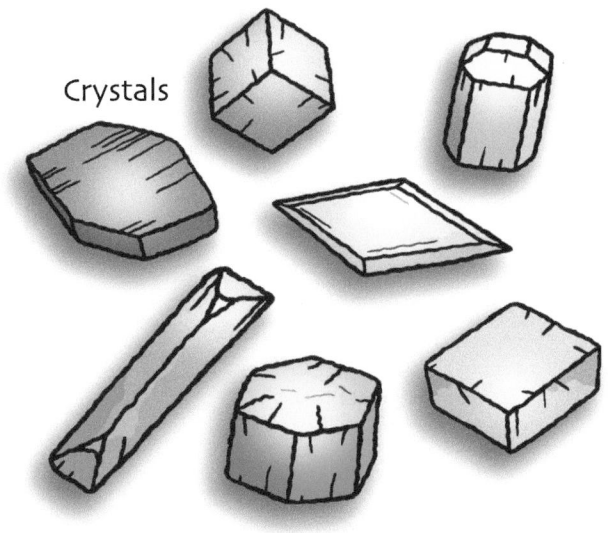

Most rocks and stones are made of a mixture of minerals with crystals of different shapes and sizes

Granite is a hard speckled looking rock made of four kinds of crystals Each speckle is a different crystal

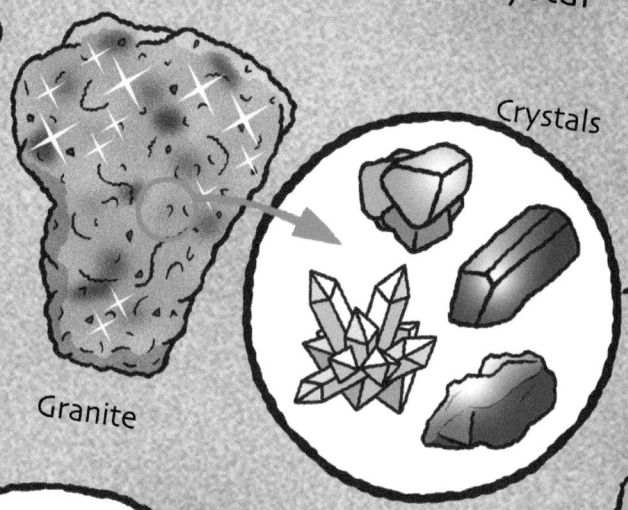

HEAR THAT? I'M A SPECIAL STONE.

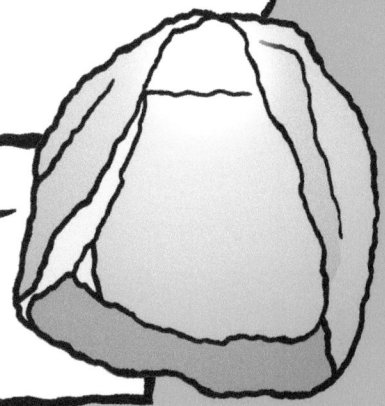

But our stone was different—its crystals were all the same They had formed from just one material called carbon This made our stone a very special stone

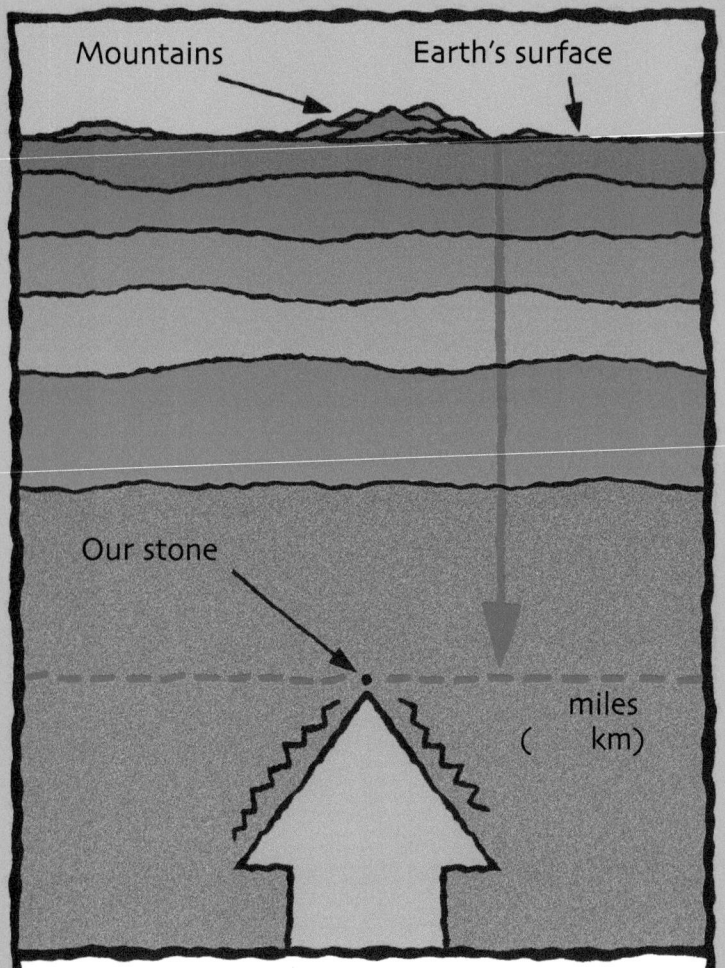

Millions more years passed and our stone moved higher up the mantle It was now about miles (kilometers) below the surface

Above the stone the mantle mixture pushed up against the crust Some of the mixture cooled and hardened and stuck to the bottom of the crust

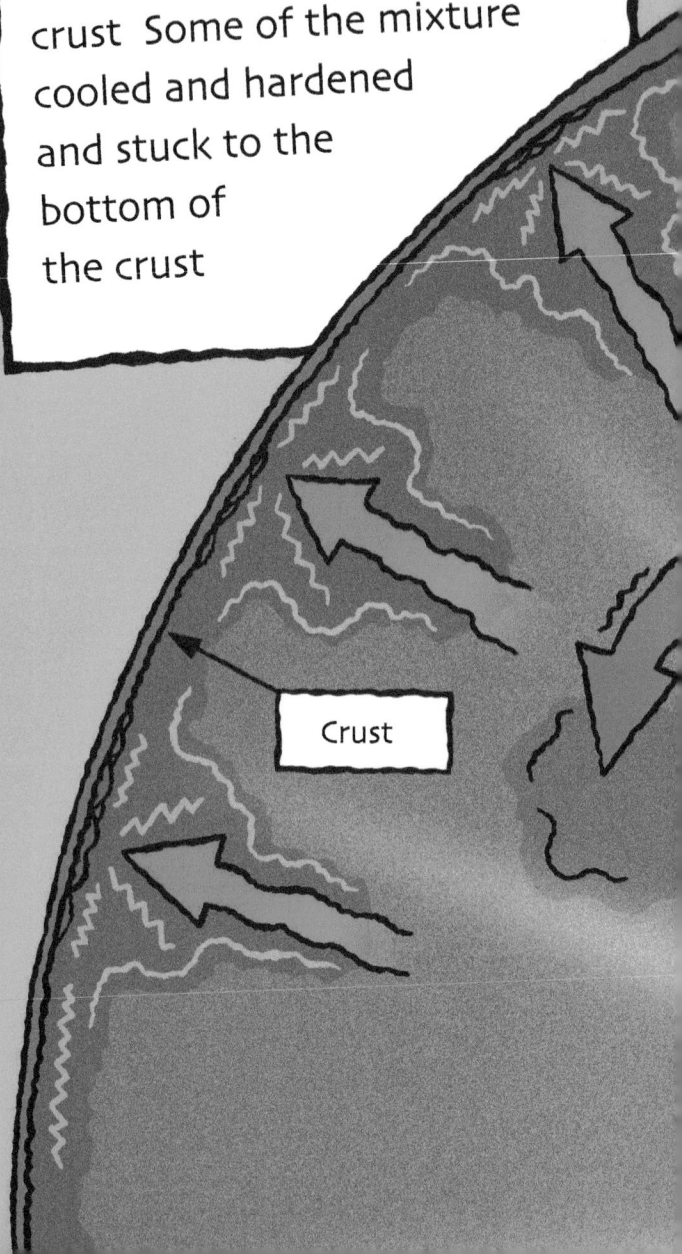

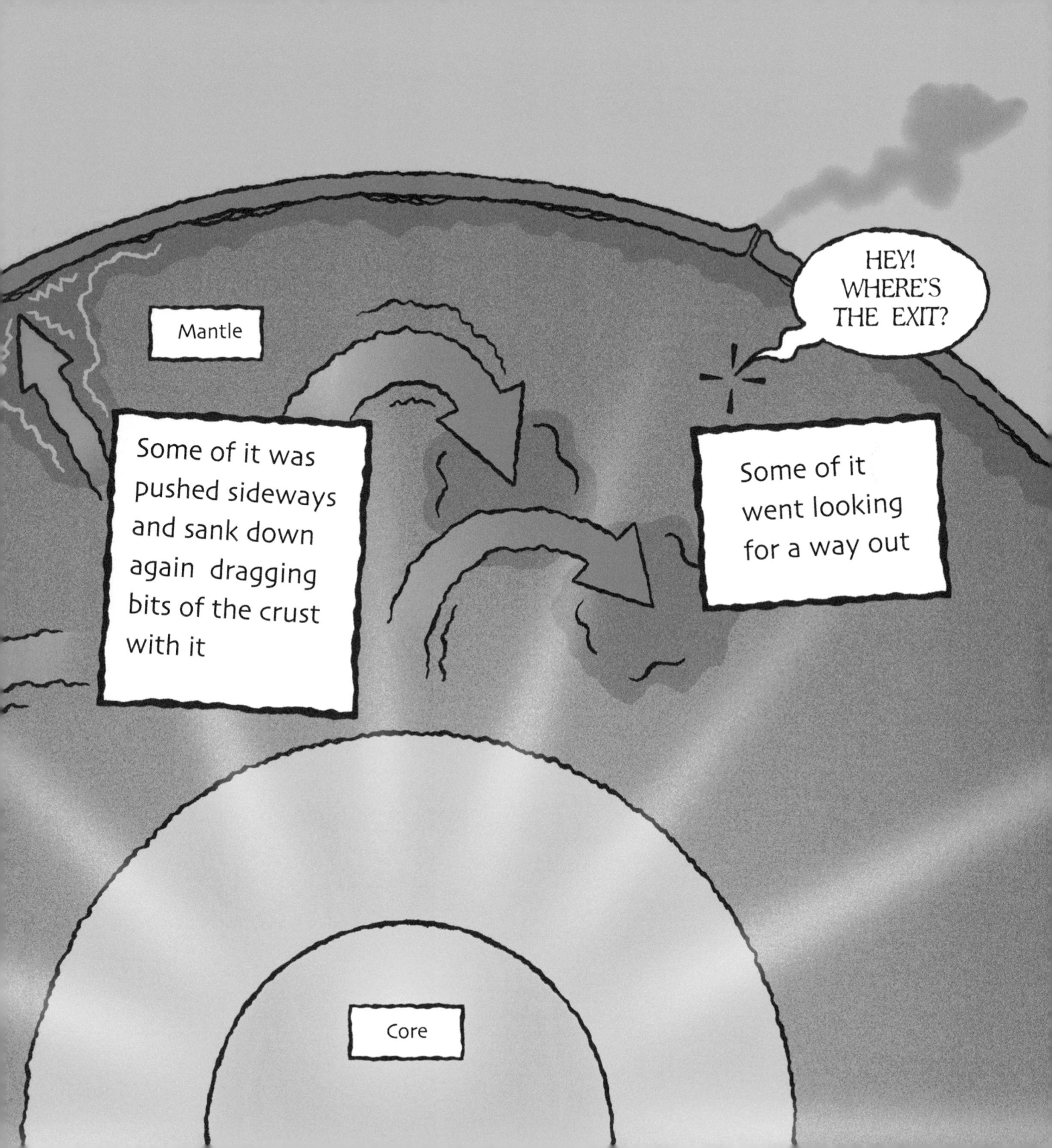
Mantle
HEY! WHERE'S THE EXIT?
Some of it was pushed sideways and sank down again dragging bits of the crust with it
Some of it went looking for a way out
Core

As the rock mixture moves up the mantle some of it softens and turns into a grainy liquid This liquid is called magma

If it finds a gap it surges into it tearing a hole right through the crust and gushing onto the surface like soda pop from a shaken bottle

Magma moves more easily through the mantle than the rest of the rock mixture When it reaches the crust it builds up underneath it Then it pushes and squeezes its way into any gaps in the crust that it can find

This is what happens in a volcano

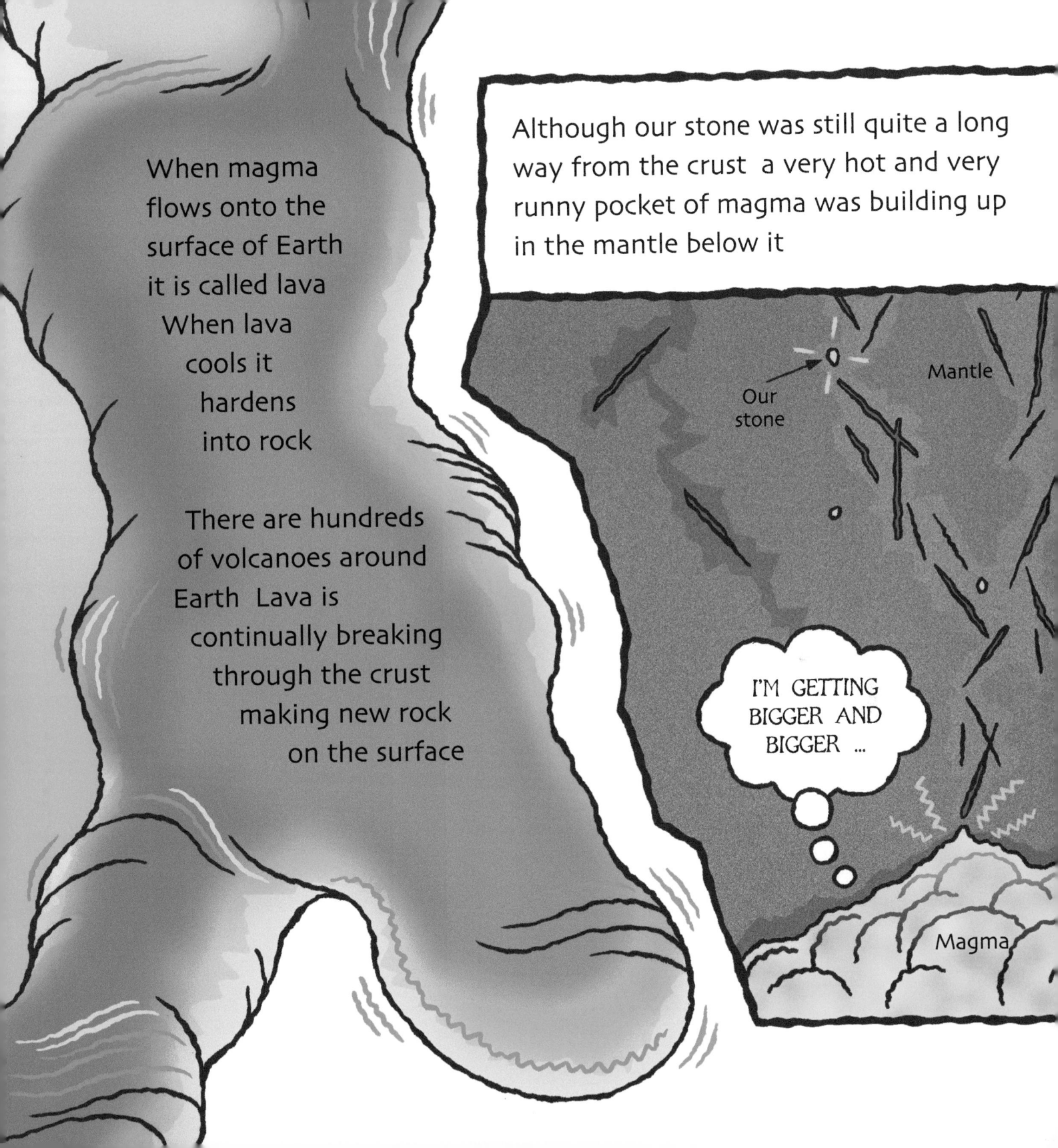
When magma flows onto the surface of Earth it is called lava When lava cools it hardens into rock
There are hundreds of volcanoes around Earth Lava is continually breaking through the crust making new rock on the surface
Although our stone was still quite a long way from the crust a very hot and very runny pocket of magma was building up in the mantle below it
Our stone
Mantle
I'M GETTING BIGGER AND BIGGER ...
Magma

The pocket of magma got bigger and bigger and instead of seeping through the mantle mixture like most magma it pushed and pushed against it

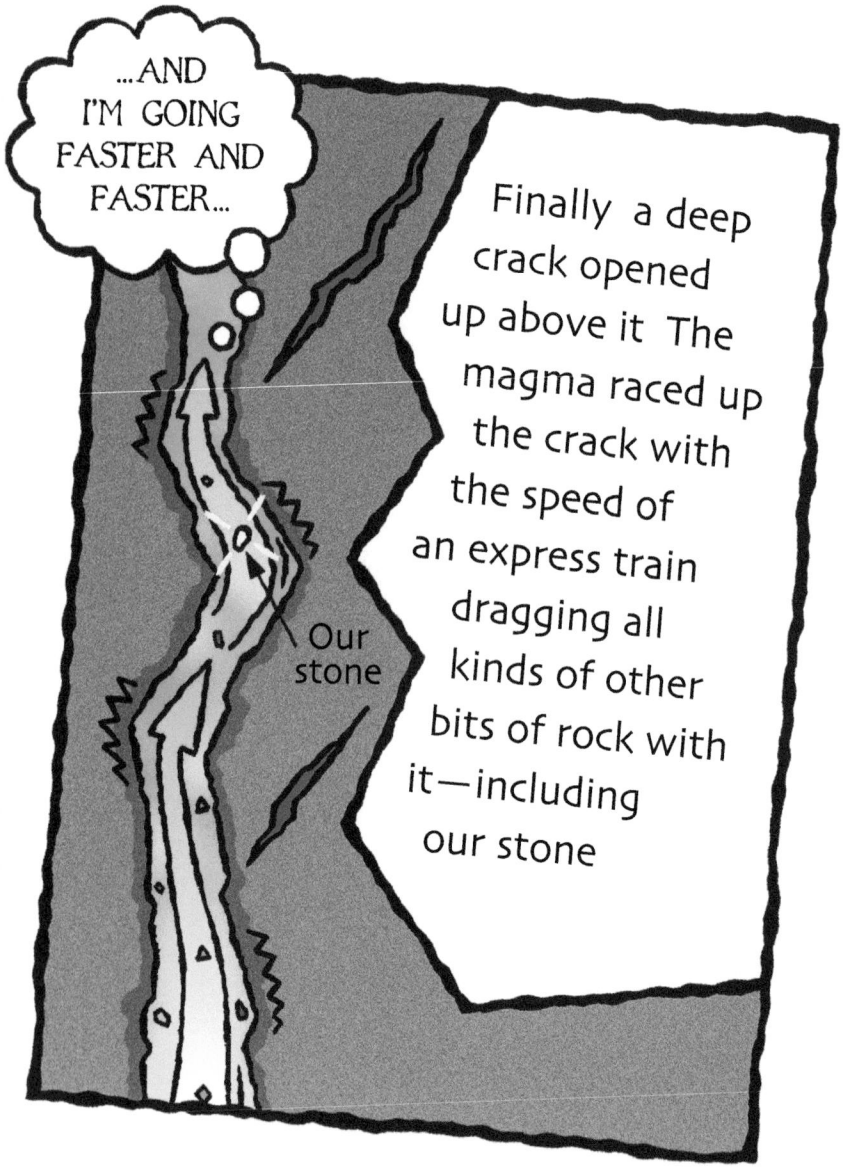

Finally a deep crack opened up above it The magma raced up the crack with the speed of an express train dragging all kinds of other bits of rock with it—including our stone

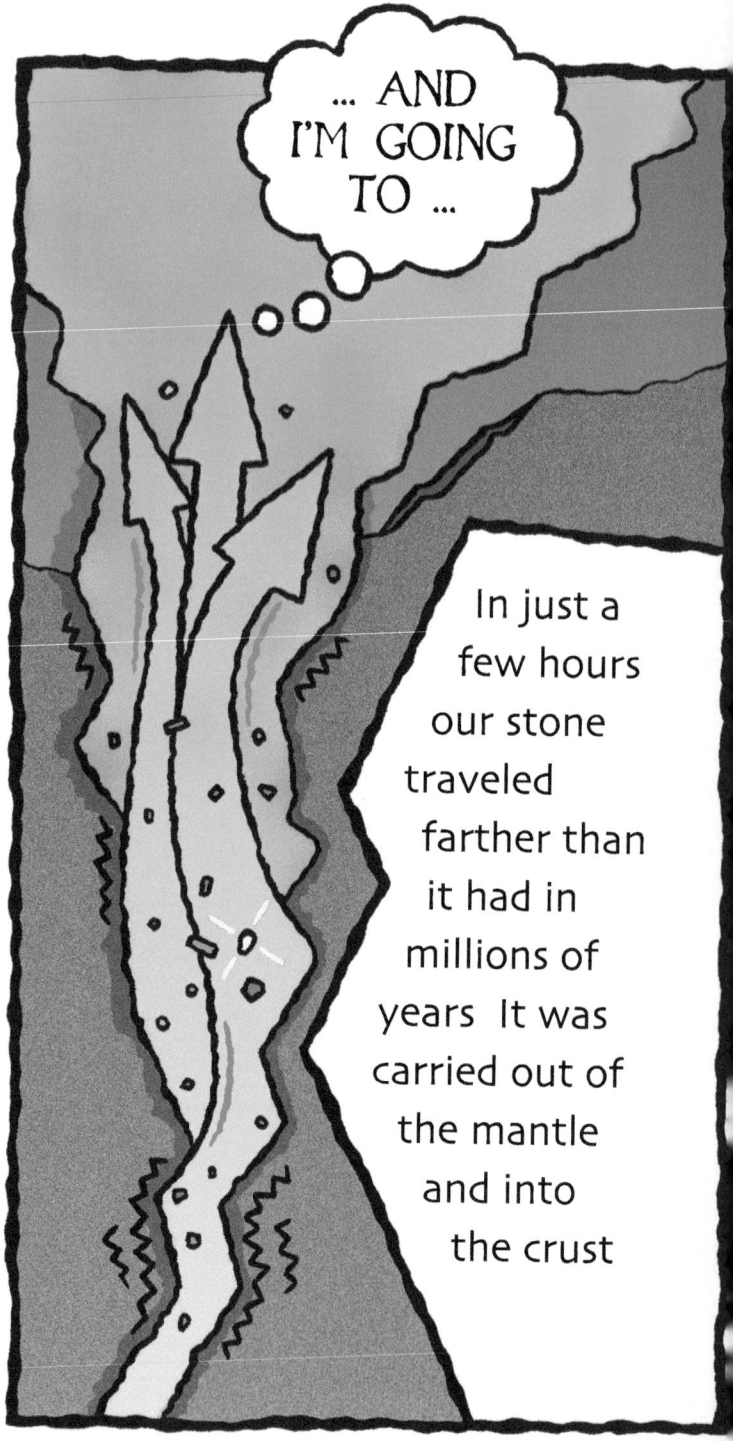

In just a few hours our stone traveled farther than it had in millions of years It was carried out of the mantle and into the crust

Up above the first wave of magma reached the surface
... EXPLODE!
The ground ripped open and a blast of scorching steam and ash exploded into the air instantly burning up anything it touched
Lumps of red hot rock and blobs of lava rained down around the volcano like a gigantic firework and our stone was brought closer and closer to the surface
Not many volcanoes are as explosive as this With some lava oozes out of the crust slowly like jelly squeezed from a doughnut

When the explosion ended there was a huge hole in the ground It looked like a giant ice cream cone filled with shattered rocks and cooling magma The stone stayed where it was

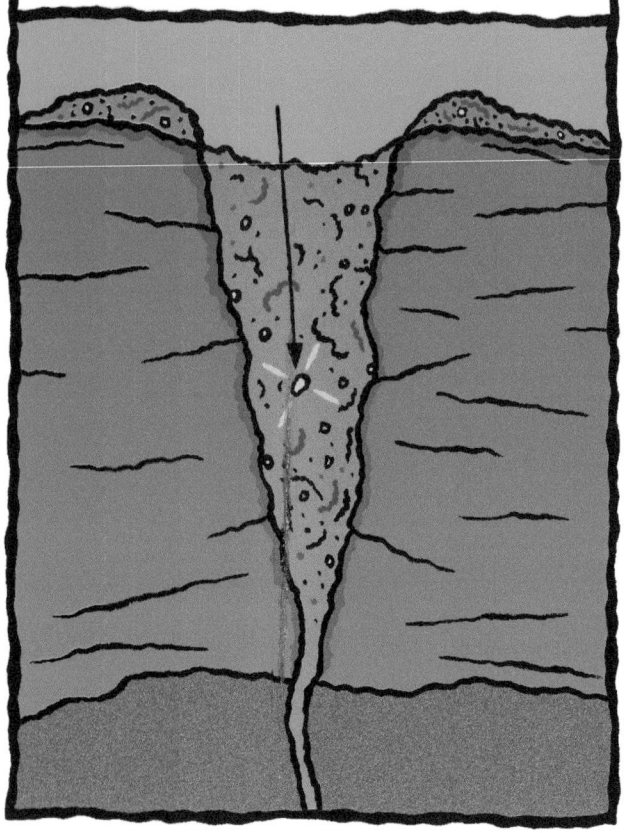

Time passed and on the surface things changed The bowl shaped top of the volcano filled with water and made a lake

Birds and other animals came to drink at the lake and trees and bushes grew around it

The wind and weather wore away at the bowl The lake overflowed and ran down the hillside to join a river far below

Over millions of years the ground around the bowl and the rock inside it were broken up into tiny pieces and washed away

One day our stone was washed away too It rolled downhill and into the river

The stone sat with other stones on the riverbed Fish nosed around it and sometimes layers of mud covered it

When animals waded into the water they churned the riverbed around The stone was rolled from place to place

One day a boy came and played by the river He dug his hands into the riverbed and pulled up a handful of wet shiny pebbles

He picked out our stone and looked at it carefully It wasn't like the other stones It was muddy and dull but it looked like a piece of glass He could almost see through it
MAYBE THIS IS A LUCKY STONE. I THINK I'LL KEEP IT.
The boy put the stone in his pocket and took it home

When the boy showed the stone to his parents they got very excited They took it to a jeweler's shop in a nearby town
HMMM! I WONDER ...

WHERE DID YOU FIND THIS?
The jeweler held the stone up to the light and peered at it closely through his magnifying glass

He reached for some tools and tried to scratch the surface of the stone but he couldn't mark it Then he measured it weighed it and wrote down some notes

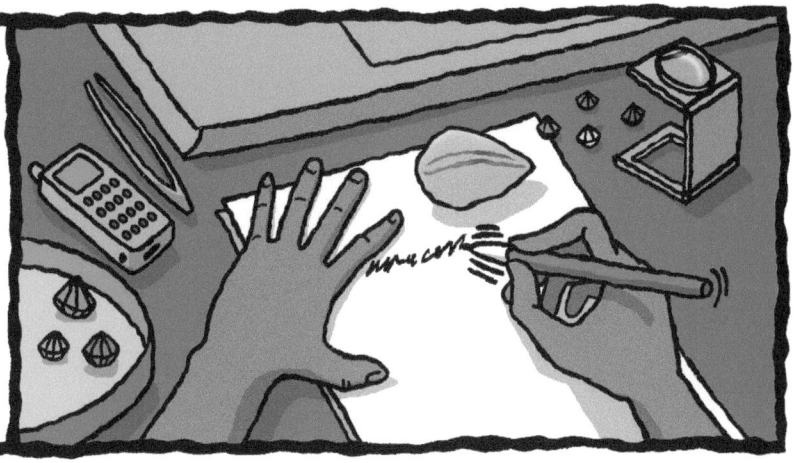

At last he looked up "You're a very lucky boy " he said

MORE GREAT STUFF TO KNOW

DIAMONDS ARE FOREVER

Diamonds are the hardest natural material in the world They can only be cut by another diamond

Diamonds are also among the oldest things on Earth They may be billion years old! But some diamonds are even older than this They are found in meteorites—chunks of rock that fall to Earth from space Meteorites can contain tiny bits of diamond up to billion years old

A COOL CRUST

Scientists think Earth formed from dust and gas whirling around the sun about billion years ago It took more than a bil lion years for Earth to cool down enough for the crust to form and the oceans to fill with water The crust is much thinner under the oceans than under the land In some places it is only about miles (km) thick Under land it can be up to miles (km) thick

Hot Rocks

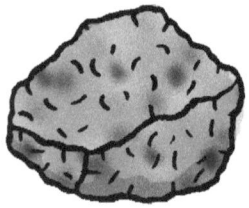

granite

Most rocks belong to one of three groups Rocks that are made when magma or lava hardens are called igneous (ig nee us) or fiery rock Granite is a type of igneous rock

Rocks that are heated or squeezed so much they turn into a different sort of rock are called metamorphic (met uh mor fik) or changed rock Marble is a metamorphic rock made from lime stone

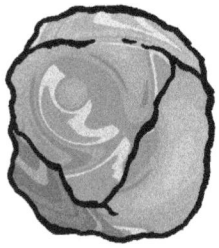

marble

Limestone belongs to the third group known as sedimentary (se da men ta ree) rock When surface rocks are worn down into tiny pieces and washed into the ocean they form layers of mud on the ocean floor Over millions of years the layers pile up until the ones at the bottom are squeezed into solid rock again

Mighty Minerals

Minerals don't only make rocks they help build our bodies too Some of the chemicals in minerals such as calcium help our bones and teeth to grow properly We get most of the minerals we need from the food we eat Farmers often add extra minerals to the soil to grow stronger and healthier plants

TRY IT AND SEE

Grow Your Own Crystals

Lots of everyday materi
als are made from crystals
Water forms crystals when it
freezes into ice Snowflakes
are tiny masses of ice
crystals Salt crystals form
when seawater dries up

Try growing your own crystals
It may take a week or so
The longer you wait the
better the crystals will be

You will need:

- A measuring cup
- Hot water
- Salt
- A teaspoon
- A wooden spoon
- Food dye (if you have it)
- A glass jar
- A pencil and some yarn

Ask an adult to boil some water and pour about / cup (ml) into the measuring cup

While the water is still hot add a teaspoon of salt and carefully stir the mixture with the wood en spoon When the salt has dissolved add another teaspoonful

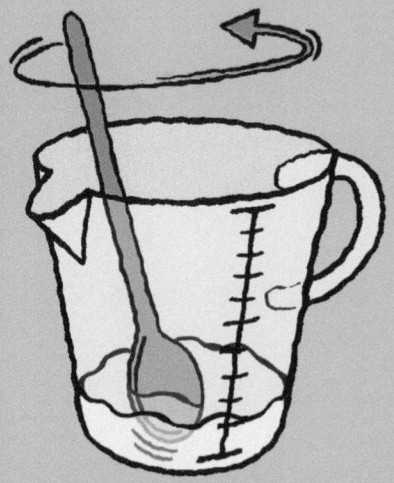

When that has dissolved add another one Keep going until the salt stops dissolving and starts to col lect in the bottom of the cup—after about teaspoons

Stir in a few drops of food dye This isn't vital but your crystals will look more interesting

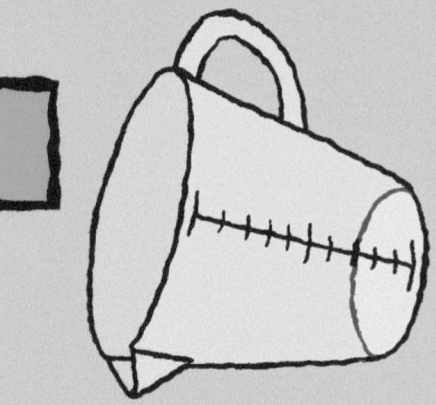

Pour the colored saltwater into the glass jar

Cut a short length of yarn and tie one end to the middle of the pencil Balance the pencil on top of the jar so that the yarn dangles into the liquid

Put your jar somewhere where it will not be disturbed Gradually the water in the jar will cool down and start to evaporate It will turn to a gas and float into the air

The remaining water will not be able to hold onto the dissolved salt any longer The salt will cling to the yarn and to the sides of the jar and form crystals

Once crystals start forming on the yarn try putting it into a fresh batch of salt water (make sure the mixture has cooled first) This encourages the crystals to grow on the yarn rather than on the sides of the jar

ROCKY FACTS

Diamond mining in South Africa began in the s when a year old boy Erasmus Jacobs found "a pebble" on the bank of a river on his father's farm It was a large diamond Today most of the world's diamonds come from mines in Australia Africa Russia and Canada

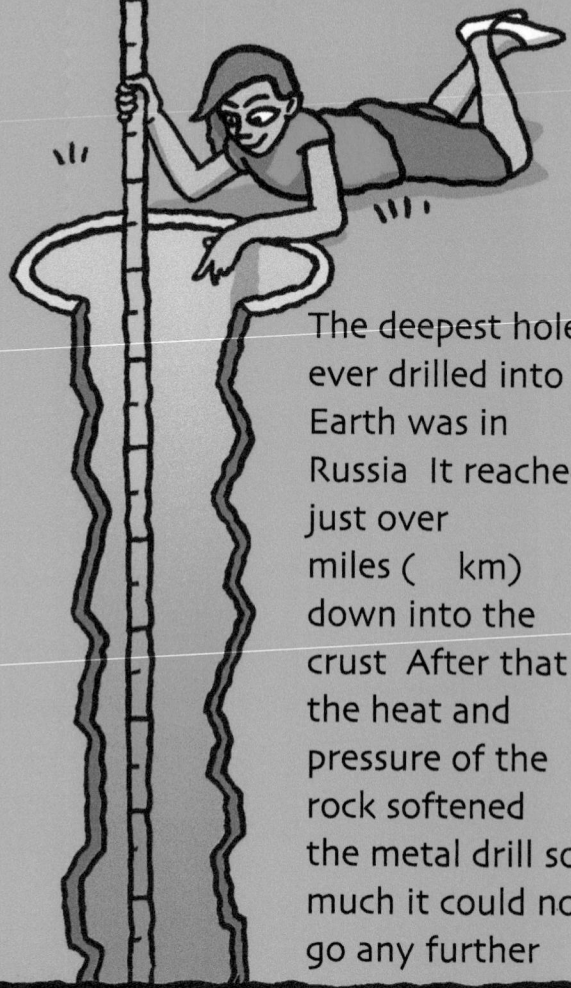

The deepest hole ever drilled into Earth was in Russia It reached just over miles (km) down into the crust After that the heat and pressure of the rock softened the metal drill so much it could not go any further

There are about active volcanoes in the world today and lots more that are sleeping or dormant Volcanoes can be dormant for thousands of years and then sud denly burst into life again

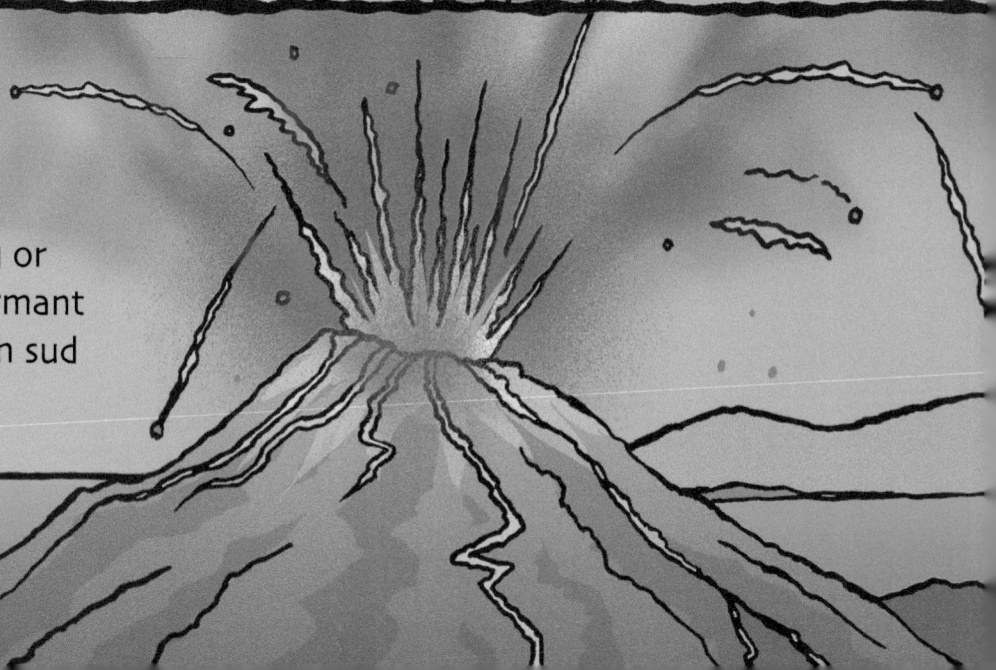

GLOSSARY

core—the inner layer of Earth

crust—the outer layer of Earth

igneous rock—rock made when hot melted rock cools down

lava—liquid rock that flows out of a volcano and hardens as it cools

limestone—hard rock that contains calcium

magma—hot melted rock beneath Earth's surface

mantle—the middle layer of Earth

metamorphic rock—rock formed by heat and pressure

minerals—the materials that make up a rock

volcano—mountains that emit hot gases and melted rock from deep within Earth

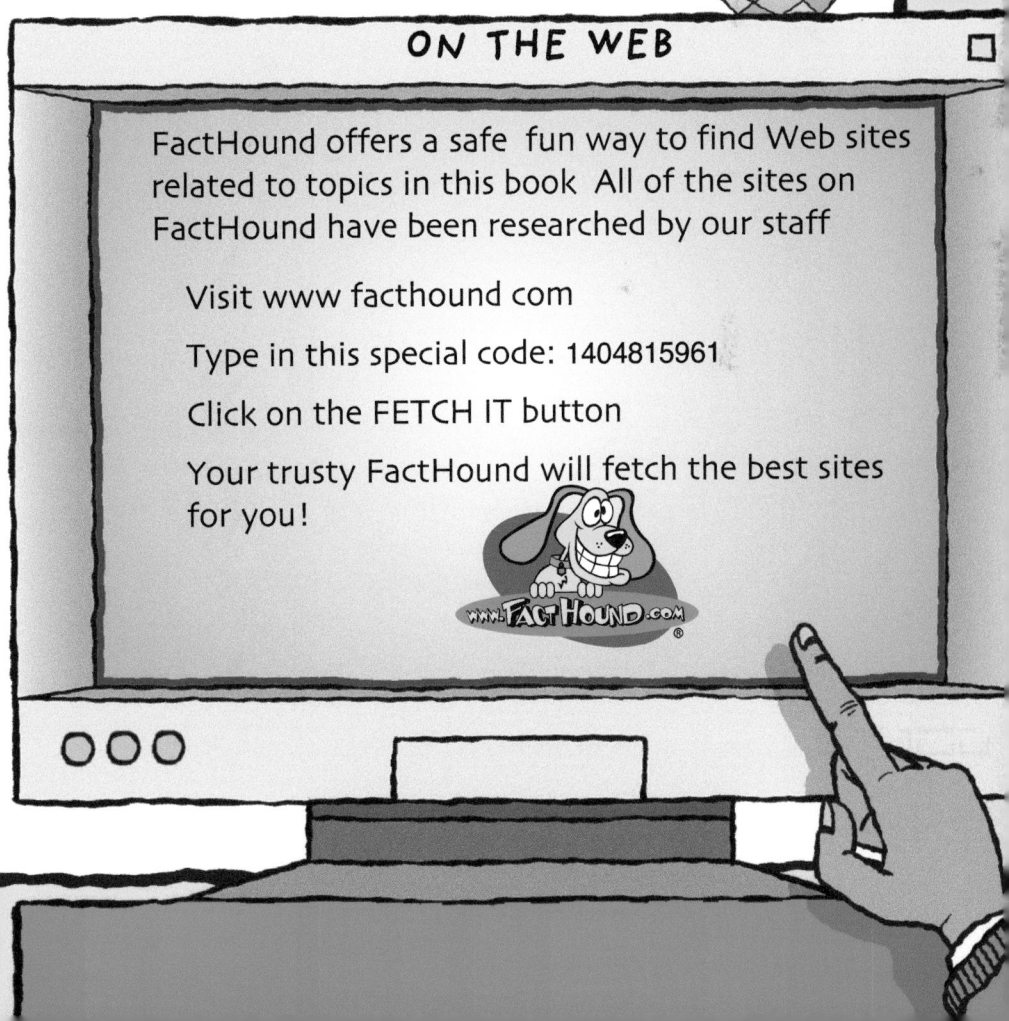

INDEX

calcium
carbon
core
crust

crystals
diamond mining
diamonds
Earth
    drilling into
    formation of
    inside
    surface of

gases
granite
igneous rocks
jeweler
land
lava
limestone
liquid rock
magma
mantle

marble
metal
metamorphic rocks

meteorites
minerals
oceans
sedimentary rocks
volcanoes

water
weather

Read all of the books in the Science Works series:

A Drop in the Ocean
The Story of Water

Charged Up
The Story of Electricity

Cracking Up
A Story About Erosion

Monster Bones
The Story of a Dinosaur Fossil

The Rock Factory
A Story of Rocks and Stones

Staying Alive
The Story of a Food Chain

Sun Up Sun Down
The Story of Day and Night

Up Down All Around
A Story of Gravity

X

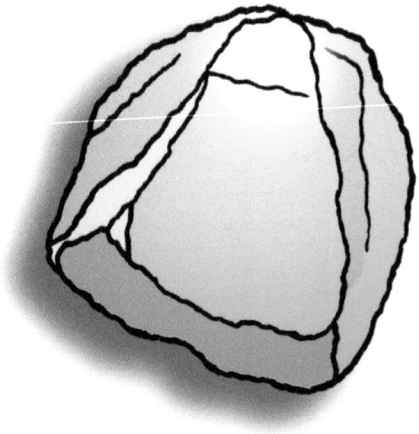